ADDITIONAL PRAISE FOR VALUE LEVERS

Value Levers is an interesting and thought-provoking read with many excellent ideas, even for an experienced guy like me whose been on one side or the other in dozens of deals, from simple asset purchases to complicated multiple-entity mergers. This is a "what-to-do guide" and has caused me to now review some of our current companies from the lenses provided. I'm convinced following these steps will increase the multiples during an ownership transition.

— Joe McKinney, President/CEO,
   McVantage Group of Companies; YPO member

"As a business owner and a thought leader in the private business marketplace, experts like Kenneth Marks give you value growth ideas that can result in a near-immediate impact. At a time when the marketplace for private companies is challenged with the largest 'value gap' I have ever seen, I highly recommend this book to any business owner or investment or transactional advisory professional."

— Michael R. Nall, CPA, CM&AA, CGMA,
   Founder, Alliance of Merger & Acquisition Advisors (AM&AA)
   and Co-Founder, MidMarket Alliance

"Kenneth Marks is one of the leading M&A professionals in the Southeast, and he and Buddy Howard have summarized in a clear and concise manner the key value drivers involved with increasing a company's valuation. This book is an excellence reference for the seasoned M&A professional and a great overview for the business owner considering an exit with no experience selling a company."

— David Kidd, Managing Partner, Adirondack Growth Capital

VALUE LEVERS

LEVERS

INCREASE THE VALUE
OF YOUR BUSINESS FROM
3X TO 7X

KENNETH H. MARKS & JOHN A. HOWARD

ISBN: 0-9705569-0-X
ISBN-13: 978-0-9705569-0-5
Library of Congress Control Number: 2016903868

Wyndham Business Press
Raleigh, North Carolina

This short book is largely based on the academic work by the authors above
and reprinted with permission: Kenneth H. Marks, John A. Howard (2015), Optimizing
Private Middle-Market Companies for M&A and Growth, in Cary L. Cooper, Sydney
Finkelstein (ed.) Advances in Mergers and Acquisitions (Advances in Mergers and
Acquisitions, Volume 14) Emerald Group Publishing Limited, pp.67 – 82.

Our work is dedicated to building God's kingdom.

CONTENTS

PREFACE

Before you embark on reading this short book, I would like to set the context for thinking about the content we are sharing. My business partner (and co-author) and I spend the vast majority of our time working with owners and CEOs of middle-market companies. In 2015, we wrote a chapter in an academic book called "Advances in Mergers & Acquisitions, Vol 14," about optimizing private middle-market companies for mergers and acquisitions (M&A) and growth. The concepts we laid out in that chapter, and in this short book, are based on years of investment banking and corporate development work coupled with our collective experience researching, writing and teaching about how to successfully finance, grow, position, buy and sell companies.

We spend a lot of our time understanding owners' ambitions and needs, and then working through corporate strategy to meet those goals. A common theme we see in our work is the need for owners to increase the value of their businesses and position them for a future transaction. Sometimes the transaction is a sale of a company, sometimes an acquisition or sometimes a financing for either growth or recapitalization. Our desire with this publication is to share our findings in a short and concise text that discusses the key levers that impact value and that might allow a company to increase the realizable multiple applied to cash flow by a buyer or investor in a transaction. The typical valuation metric used in these kinds of deals is a multiple of earnings before interest, taxes, depreciation and amortization (EBITDA); the ideas in this book have the potential to move the EBITDA multiple from 3x to 7x.

Hopefully, this short book will spur your thinking and provide some high-level guidance to get you started or to move you closer to reaching your or your clients' objectives. To further help, we are building-out tools and content for your use at www.ValueLevers.net. As always, we are open to discussion, feedback or questions.

Kenneth H. Marks, CM&AA, CFq
Managing Partner at High Rock Partners, Inc.
khmarks@HighRockPartners.com
(919) 256-8152

INTRODUCTION

For private, middle-market companies—those companies with annual revenues from $5 million to $1 billion—value creation is principally based on long-term, expected future cash flow. In practice, the activities that lead to value creation are nearly the same when preparing for a financing, a wave of growth or an M&A transaction.

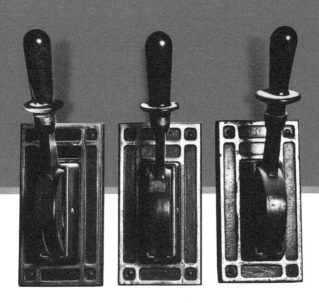

Owners of private companies tend to manage the business to minimize taxes and maximize the current cash benefit to the shareholders. While this approach makes sense in the short term, it often over-weights decisions and strategies for immediate impact at the expense of what outside investors or lenders would consider long-term value creation. Many times, improving the realizable value of a company means shifting its approach and stance from one that is reactive to one that is proactive. Taking a proactive stance means, among other things, a company will tackle tough issues and instill disciplines like those in which an institutional investor would insist. A useful question for management to ask in readying their company for change is "What would a private equity buyer do to improve my business?" The answer to that question will likely provide keen insights and areas of focus. That is what we hope to provide in this short book.

Essential to increasing the value of a company is increasing the amount and certainty of its cash flow while reducing the risk of achieving that cash flow. Optimizing the business should result in both a shift in the market value of the company towards the upper end of valuation benchmarks and an increase in its alternatives (more buyers, cheaper capital, etc.) when engaging with the capital markets. Our discussion here centers on those value levers most critical to the optimization of private, middle-market companies from the perspective of those in the capital markets, including institutional investors, lenders and buyers.

As we begin this analysis, keep in mind that strategic decisions need to be thought of and developed by aligning the company's long-term growth strategy with the right leadership team and the appropriate entity and organizational structure supported by scalable systems, and capitalized by the proper funding sources. Management must also consider changes to a company relative to its stage and lifecycle within its specific market.

Calculating the value of a stream of cash flow can be illustrated in mathematic terms by this simplified formula[1].

$$VALUE = \frac{expected\ cash\ flow}{cost\ of\ capital - growth\ rate\ of\ the\ cash\ flow}$$

[1] There are variations of this formula that account for fast-growth businesses, and for those with negative short-term cash flow and positive long-term cash flow. Further explanation of this formula is provided at the back of the book.

According to this equation, we can increase value by increasing the absolute value of the cash flow, reducing the cost of capital or increasing the rate of growth of the cash flow (or any combination of the three). Reducing the cost of capital is, in part, directly related to the risk of achieving that cash flow. To frame the discussion and apply some basic corporate finance concepts, we will look at value creation and optimization of a private, middle-market company as an exercise with three distinct types of value levers: (i) pursuit of strategies that increase the return on invested capital, (ii) pursuit of strategies that reduce the risk of investment in the company, and (iii) pursuit of tactics and strategies that ease the transfer and reduce the company's specific risk of transitioning a business to new owners (whether transferred in part or in whole).

Keep in mind that certain businesses don't generate positive cash flow in the early phase of their lifecycle but do create significant inherent value. From a buyer or investor perspective, these companies may have captured (or are capturing) a significant customer base or developing a technology that will eventually lead to relatively large and material cash flows. The discussion and concepts in this short book still apply.

Lastly, strategic position is an important lever that is discussed in both the first and second chapters.

Visit www.ValueLevers.net for additional content and tools.

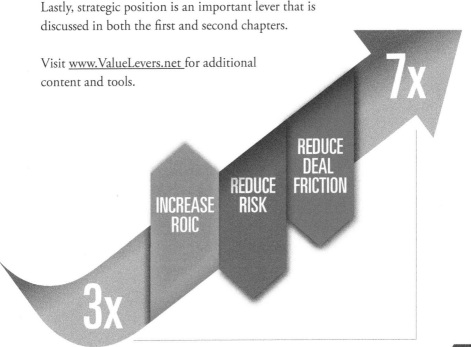

INCREASING
THE RETURN
ON INVESTED CAPITAL

INCREASING THE RETURN ON INVESTED CAPITAL

One of the common ways to measure return on invested capital (ROIC) is to divide (i) net operating profit less adjusted taxes by (ii) total assets minus non-interest bearing liabilities (Copeland, 1996)[2].

$$ROIC = \frac{operating\ profit\ -\ adjusted\ taxes}{total\ assets\ -\ non\text{-}interest\ bearing\ debt}$$

To increase the ROIC, a company can either increase its operating profits and cash flow while maintaining the same level of invested capital, or it can reduce the amount of invested capital while maintaining the same operating profit and cash flow. Under ideal circumstances, management will do both simultaneously.

Below we discuss five key levers that can work to manage, control and increase the ROIC. The primary outcome of moving these levers should be increased cash flow and improved capital efficiency; however, a possible, secondary effect of moving these levers is an increase in the rate of growth of that cash flow. Preparation for growth or for an M&A transaction includes developing and prioritizing appropriate initiatives to optimize the ROIC of the company given the risk profile and ambitions of the shareholders. As a company optimizes its ROIC, it is likely to also experience improved operating metrics, such as better-than-industry-average gross and EBITDA margins, and faster growth as compared to its peers, both of which contribute to greater value.

[2] Further explanation of this formula is provided at the back of the book.

1 Strategic Position

The strategic position of a company is essentially its competitive stance relative to its peers and industry or market segment. Ideally, the better a company's strategic position, the greater its ability to win and maintain business and add value for its customers. At a minimum, management should (i) understand the market and the company's competitive position, and (ii) evidence and validate the company's relative position. Third-party validation is often helpful in addressing both of the these. For example, being recognized in specialized industry or segment reports that highlight a company can be useful, assuming the company is in a strong position. Industry awards and recognition are another means to validate strategic position. A company in a weak or average position may need to implement initiatives to create a stronger position or reposition to a sustainable posture.

In today's world, few companies can thrive in a vacuum, so creating a network of alliances or partnerships can help to gain advantage in a marketplace. Alliances or partnerships might provide cost or supply advantages, unique capabilities, desired sales channels or access to technologies that competitors can't easily duplicate. These relationships can improve the competitive position of a company and provide evidence of the value of that company, particularly if the alliance or partnership is with a recognizable industry player. Ideally, a company's strategic position will logically fit and address the industry or sector trends and play into them in a way that is advantageous going forward. Whether the company's strategic position has recently emerged, has slowly evolved or is well entrenched, being able to articulate and leverage that position is an important part of the growth story and the foundation upon which to build an operating strategy.

2 Customer Base

The competitive and strategic position of a business is linked to its go-forward customer base. As a company transitions from one stage of growth to another, the customer base evolves. A goal in optimizing the value of the business at the time of a transaction is to establish a customer base that appreciates the value the company provides and is willing to pay for it. Does the company have a customer base it can build upon and grow? Do these customers fit the profile of what can be thought of as ideal customers?

Since buyers or investors are paying for future cash flow, they will pay significant attention to the quality of revenues, earnings and cash flow. The strength of a company's customer base – which obviously is the driver of revenues and, therefore, cash flow – can greatly influence the quality of earnings/cash flow and how well those earnings represent future projections based on the strategy of the business. The process of improving the quality of revenues and earnings may very well include culling customers that are problematic, low margin, slow paying, or that are otherwise consuming resources or products/services that aren't core to the future of the business and replacing these customers with those that more closely fit the ideal profile. To improve the value of the business is to more tightly align the customer base with the growth strategy, giving it a higher quality of revenues and earnings.

3 Cost Structure & Scalability

As with the customer base, the operations of a company should be configured in the context of its overall growth strategy. From a buyer or investor perspective, these decisions could include outsourcing non-core activities, automating processes, optimizing the mix of contract vs. permanent employees and improving utilization of facilities. Any of these changes can have an impact on the cost of goods and services, research and development, sales, general and administrative expenses, and they should be synchronized with the growth strategy and the stage of the company.

To create operating leverage, management might explore how the structure of a specific operating area or capability within the company could allow the business to ramp-up its revenues and output disproportionally to the required investment or expense. The greater the disproportionality, the greater the scalability implied, particularly where the contribution margin of incremental revenues grows as the business grows. With a high-growth business, this scalability would likely be seen as creating additional enterprise value. Some software companies, for example, have transitioned away from the traditional enterprise model and adopted a software-as-a-service model, in which a significant number of new customers can be added with relatively minimal new costs, creating a dramatic impact to valuation. This is one of the reasons that companies such as Facebook have such high valuations; customer acquisition is often self-perpetuating, and the incremental cost is close to zero.

4 Working Capital

In accounting terms, working capital is equal to current assets minus current liabilities. In middle-market M&A transactions (those beyond the small, Main Street asset deals), the selling company is typically expected to deliver a normalized level of working capital to support the operations of the business post-closing. Calculating the working capital and figuring the basis for the analysis is somewhat of an art and often changes depending on the norms of a specific industry. Historical trends can be a sound baseline for establishing the target amount. The argument that a buyer can operate the seller's company with less working capital than the seller is hard to defend without evidence. In growth financings, tightening the working capital cycle can provide a cheap and quickly accessed source of funding. In both M&A and growth financing, optimizing the working capital cycle and assuring efficient use of this capital will increase the value of the business by decreasing or minimizing the capital required to fund the operating cycle.

Modifying the working capital cycle within a company can touch many aspects of the business. The approach and ability to make these changes depends, in some part, on the relative strategic and competitive strength of the company and the desirability of its products or services. This is where we connect the dots from the discussions above. Typical ways to tighten the working capital cycle include accelerating customer payment or requiring pre-payment, extending supplier credit terms to market norms, increasing inventory turns and reducing the overall operating or process cycle times.

When a seller in an M&A transaction tightens the working capital cycle a number of quarters prior to a sale, he or she demonstrates that the new norm is sustainable. From a buyer's perspective, this tightened working capital cycle can reduce the risk associated with estimations when negotiating the working capital target.

5 Human Capital

Engaging and developing the human resources of a company is the final lever to highlight in our discussion about increasing the return on invested capital. In fact, human capital is often the greatest investment a business makes. To realize the highest value for this investment, management should focus on three interrelated areas: continuous improvement, incentives and culture. A company's ability to grow and thrive is directly linked to its ability to attract, retain and reward employees while engendering a sense of ownership and accomplishment at all levels. When optimized, the integration of these three areas should result in a culture of innovation, reduced costs, improved operating efficiencies and the institutionalization of the knowledge and wisdom of the business into the processes and systems of the organization (Sanginario, 2014).

REDUCING THE RISK
OF INVESTMENT

REDUCING THE RISK OF INVESTMENT

Risk is defined as the variability of an expected return over time (Damodaran, 1999). Once a buyer or investor has bought into the company's growth story or established an investment thesis and determined the potential outcomes are within an acceptable range, the focus of the analysis turns to risk mitigation and sharing, that is, sharing the risks between the buyer and seller for a period of time beyond closing the deal. Proactively reducing or mitigating these risks can allow management to increase the value of the company. A reduction in the risks of the business should result in a reduced cost of capital or lower expected variability from the target return on investment and, thus, greater implied value in the cash flow. This leads the owner to pursue strategies that reduce the risk of investment in the company.

In practice, lowering perceived risks helps establish and build confidence throughout the transaction process and decreases discounts or hedging by the buyer or investor in pricing the business. The goal is to demonstrate the possible value streams (which will eventually become cash flow) generated by acquisition of or investment in the company and to provide indicators that build confidence and increase the certainty of achieving them.

In this discussion around risk, remember that private, middle-market companies are not managed in the same way as public and larger businesses. In private, middle-market companies, non-financial owner and shareholder ambitions directly impact managements' actions and willingness to confront tough situations or make changes that might otherwise make logical or strategic sense. Oftentimes, difficult situations are not addressed until a change of ownership or a crisis spurs improvement. In fact, the need to make tough decisions often drives the change of ownership. The proactive acknowledgement of this dynamic in itself can set the stage for releasing unrealized value within a company, if not by making tough decisions, then by understanding what the difficult decisions are and presenting the investment opportunity as part of the solution. To a buyer or investor, inheriting hard decisions and change management activities is risky and will likely reduce the realizable value of the company. It is good practice, therefore, to reduce a company's risk prior to a transaction by implementing changes that address its critical challenges or issues.

The following discussion highlights some of the key areas of risk that tend to surface in mergers, acquisitions and financings of private, middle-market companies and outlines initiatives or actions that can be taken to reduce those risks and increase the value of the enterprise.

1 Awareness and Planning

Few companies have fully optimized operations. As companies move through their lifecycle, their risks and opportunities change, so the task of managing risk is always in a state of flux. The first step in reducing the risk of buying or investing in a company is to understand the risks inherent in the type of business and the market in which it operates. The second step is to understand the distinct risks specific to the individual company. A combined understanding provides the basis for assessing the overall risk profile and for plotting a path forward. During the transaction process, the price and deal terms can hinge on management's ability to clearly articulate what is being purchased or invested in and to demonstrate a house truly in order. As mentioned above, management that is aware of and acting to mitigate the risks of the business can provide some comfort to outsiders who may have concern about undisclosed or latent issues.

2 Growth Plans and Relative Position

Understanding and optimizing a company's strategic position can provide the focus for important operating decisions. Improved positioning relative to competition should increase long-term cash flow and reduce risk as it relates to the company's relevance in its market. A breakout strategy is part of the answer to the question of a company's current and future relevance. At the minimum, a company should understand its growth scenario as a standalone entity. To create a breakout strategy, a company needs to understand its potential growth in the context of an acquisition or with a significant infusion of capital. While the standalone scenario should show sustainable growth based on the company's current capitalization and earnings, a well-thought-out and validated breakout strategy can be used as a negotiating lever for extracting additional value for a company beyond what its current cash flow might justify. For example, a company planning significant geographic expansion as its break-out strategy – a strategy that requires capital or resources to fully implement – will want to have actually expanded on its own, in at least a small way, to demonstrate the scalability of the business. Further successful expansion could be the basis for earn-out or milestone payments in the context of a sale of the company.

3 Leadership Team

In evaluating and reducing the risk related to the leadership and management of a company, one must look first at the organization's dependence on the CEO, owner or entrepreneur and then at the organization's bench strength. A company with a hands-on CEO who makes all the decisions supported by functional managers is usually riskier than a company led by a CEO who operates among a team of leaders with individual decision-making authority and that is accountable to near real-time performance metrics. From a macro perspective, a qualitative assessment can be made by answering a few core questions:

- Is the current leadership team organizationally healthy, functioning and capable of growing the business to the next level?

- Have key relationships with suppliers and customers been developed with multiple members of the leadership team?

- Has the team developed a positive culture and organization that learns and improves?

- Have any of the key members of this team experienced or led a company through this type of growth and operated at the next level?

- Are members of this team functionally learning on the job or do any have domain and industry experience?

- How successful has the team been in attracting, developing and retaining others?

- Has this team operated successfully together through a difficult time or situation?

- What has been the recent performance of the company under the leadership of this team?

- Is there an incentive for the team to perform and stay with the company beyond a transaction?

Developing a leadership team that enables a positive response to these questions and that can operate the company without need of any specific individual generally reduces the risk of investment in that company.

This kind of leadership and management assessment will resonate with most institutional investors, lenders and buyers. Nonetheless, many private owners will make the argument that it is riskier for them to hand off responsibility than to directly supervise or perform sensitive functions, such as cash management, key customer relations and large project management (Blees, 2014). This divergence of perception and the practical implications that result can contribute to a valuation gap.

4 Predictability of Revenues and Earnings

Historical financial performance is no guarantee of the future cash flow of a company, but it does provide evidence about the company's level of operating performance and management's ability to lead. Generally, predictable revenues and earnings are considered to have greater value and less risk than cyclical, seasonal or sporadic performance. The business model of a company often dictates the risk associated with predictability. For example, recurring or repeat, multi-year, contractual relationships that are likely to continue over the long-term and that can be forecasted are most desirable.

A bottoms-up revenue and expense forecast built on historical operating performance and metrics tends to inspire confidence and allows a buyer or investor to understand the value drivers of the business and the associated risks. Future revenues and earnings evidenced by contracts and existing relationships are often less risky than revenues and earnings based on individual new sales from a broad market or new customers. An example of a business between these two extremes is one with a history of sales operations that documents how certain business or selling activities directly correlate to certain customer responses and, in turn, lead to certain types or amounts of new orders. While this provides a proven and documented process for obtaining new business, revenue is generated order by order. To reduce this type of risk, this business might move to longer-term, well-defined contracts that provide backlog and visibility.

Of the various lenses for evaluating elements of the operating costs and structure, one is based on the variability of costs and its impact to the break-even level, especially for businesses that are seasonal or have episodic revenues. A company that can manage through revenue fluctuations and generate predictable earnings and cash flow is less risky than one with higher fixed costs and less control of its performance.

5 Concentrations

Customer concentration, the phenomenon of a single customer contributing a significant volume of revenues and/or consuming a large amount of the company's capacity, is generally considered to be a risk to a company's cash flow stability and, ultimately, longevity. The level at which concentration becomes an issue can change based on industry and circumstances, though twenty percent or more of annual revenues by one customer is likely to trigger a closer look. A similar risk exists with supplier concentration, especially where few alternatives exist for a critical resource. Having a long-term contract with strong protective and termination clauses with a significant customer can mitigate the risk of concentration. An even better solution to customer concentration is to obtain more customers and balance the mix of business. Supplier concentration can be mitigated by securing long-term contracts that provide for committed resources or products, finding a second source of supply or obtaining a co-right of some type (e.g. co-right of production, ownership or sourcing).

Similar to the earlier mention in this book, this perspective of risk will resonate with most institutional investors, lenders and buyers. However, many business owners will argue that concentration within a few established customers and suppliers where deeply entrenched relationships are formed is less risky than diversification, and may enable them to optimize their business' performance (Blees, 2014). Again, this divergence of perception, and the practical implications that result, is another factor that contributes to a valuation gap.

6 Compliance

Unresolved compliance issues involving taxation, payroll and benefits, labor laws and environmental regulations can indirectly impact the risk and value of a company by increasing doubt or decreasing confidence in management's ability or integrity. Direct impact to the value of a transaction is usually carved out or indemnified separately. Compliance issues often lead to valuation issues when they impact operating costs and earnings. By proactively identifying compliance issues and then developing corrective action plans that contain and resolve the issues, you can begin the process of managing risk. In some cases, the company will be better off if it resolves compliance issues before engaging in the transaction process.

7 Keeping Current

Some businesses require heavy, ongoing investment to remain relevant and growing. The need to make critical improvements in a business can create uncertainty and risk for a buyer or investor and, in some cases, can be a catalyst for a transaction. Companies that require significant investment to stay current or to update in terms of technology, facilities or equipment are often penalized in a transaction in two ways: (i) the required change is seen as creating additional risk, and (ii) the cash required to make the improvement to the company (beyond a normal level of reinvestment) impacts the value attributed to the seller. This situation is often found in companies that are undercapitalized, have failed to earn a return great enough to reinvest or stay current, or in which the owners have stripped the company of its capital and failed to reinvest. Understanding the cause of the failure to remain current in operations or products may allow management to develop a strategy for addressing it; the eventual solution will differ depending upon the cause.

The company's ability to innovate is directly related to the concepts above in assessing the risk of the enterprise. Is the company built on a single product, technology or service? Or does it have a track record of successfully responding to market changes and opportunities that provide for longevity, sustainability and continued relevance? The risk imputed for innovation, or the lack thereof, will depend on the specifics of the company, the market in which it operates and the needs of the buyer or investor.

EASING THE TRANSFER
OF OWNERSHIP

EASING THE TRANSFER OF OWNERSHIP

Optimizing the value and preparing for M&A transactions and growth, which often include external financings, may include addressing administrative and entity-related issues that cause friction in the deal process and effectively increase the risk of closing a transaction. The final concept to address in our analysis is, therefore, "greasing the skids for a transaction" and enabling management to increase the ease of, and reduce the risk of, a transfer of a company's ownership (in whole or in part). The following discussion outlines the typical sources of friction in a transaction and the techniques to improve the likelihood of accomplishing the desired deal.

1 Financial Information

The standard for financial reporting and information used for valuation is usually accrual accounting that complies with the generally accepted accounting principles (GAAP) or the international financial reporting standards (IFRS), depending on the country and agreed-upon basis for the transaction. Financial statements prepared for tax and management reporting purposes often fail to fully meet these standards, particularly in the lower middle-market. A key way to prepare in advance for engaging with the capital markets is to compile financial information, both historical and prospective, that allows the parties to directly compare data and that complies with GAAP or IFRS. Typical financial reporting problem areas include: revenue recognition, year-end payroll and benefit accruals, asset expensing vs. depreciation and normalization adjustments accounting for specific owner-related benefits.

The objective of preparing financial information is to generate numbers that allow direct comparison of revenue, gross margin, expenses, capital expenditures (CAPEX) and EBITDA amounts and percentages within the conventions of the specific company's industry. For a business with critical mass or size, having audited or reviewed financial statements from a credible and recognized accounting firm is important and, in some cases, required. Even with reviewed or audited statements in hand, many parties involved in M&A and financing transactions require an additional, external assessment of the timing and value of cash flow of the business, which is often referred to as a quality-of-earnings assessment.

Since value creation is based on future cash flow, it is important to note that capturing, evaluating and optimizing the true economics of a business includes understanding the required future investment in CAPEX. Though this investment is often excluded from traditional EBITDA metrics, it can have a significant impact that needs to be understood to drive value growth. In addition to traditional financial reporting, key performance measures, leading indicators and operating data and metrics provide valuable insight into business operations and allow management (and new owners) to react and adapt to changes (Blees, 2014).

Having well-organized and accurate financial information allows the parties to move deliberately and quickly through the analysis, decision and negotiating phases of the deal and supports the momentum and energy that builds as a transaction process advances.

2 Contracts

One determinant of the ease of transfer of a business is the ease of assignment of its contracts from one owner to another. For businesses with long-term customer contracts, agreements that are assignable and that don't require a change of control consent by the customer allow flexibility in determining the deal structure and reduce the risk of disrupting customer relationships during the transition. This assignability challenge is sometimes alleviated when there is a stock transaction, since the company continues to exist post-closing. The same concept applies to various other contracts that a company might have, including employee agreements, supplier contracts, facilities leases, licensing agreements and debt instruments. Based on the industry, size and stage of growth of the company, management should consider the type of transactions that might benefit its shareholders and shape its agreements accordingly.

3 Title to Assets

At some point in the process of completing an M&A transaction or obtaining growth financing, the topic of defining and listing the assets of a business will arise. This requires identifying both tangible assets (e.g., property, plant and equipment) and intangible assets (e.g., software, trademarks, patents, trade secrets and customer lists). Understanding what a company owns and how much those assets are worth are factors in determining the structure of a transaction and how purchase price is allocated (which impacts taxes for both the buyer and seller). A step in preparing for a transaction is to develop a comprehensive list of a company's assets and establish and provide evidence of clear title. This may involve having liens removed from public records. For intellectual property (IP), it may require filings, registrations, releases or assignments depending on the circumstances in which the IP was created. As with other areas of preparation, working through the details of this step can take time. Waiting until the time of a transaction to act can slow the process and increase costs of a deal.

Corporate Structure and Attributes

Two common topics that arise when considering the legal entity and structure of a transaction and the interaction with selling shareholders (or members) are: (i) tax treatment of the selling entity and (ii) approvals by the seller required to affect a transaction.

i. Optimizing after-tax proceeds from M&A transactions usually requires long-term planning regarding the seller's type of corporate entity and its tax status. Determining if, when, why and with whom a company is likely to engage in the capital markets can provide some guidance as to whether C-corp or S-corp (or partnership if an LLC) status makes sense for optimizing the value to its owners over time. Changing status on short notice is usually punitive and might create practical barriers or negate the economic value as the motivation for a deal, especially for transactions with companies that have marginal performance.

ii. For entities with multiple owners with divergent levels of interest, having clear authority to execute a transaction can be valuable in preventing delays. A typical approach to control is for the majority shareholder(s) to create a formal shareholder agreement (or operating agreement for LLCs) that provides for drag-along rights of minority owners. Another approach is to plan ahead and buyout the minority, disgruntled or estranged shareholders well before a transaction is imminent.

5 Don't Lose Focus on the Core Business

A word of caution: it is important for management to remain focused on company performance while engaging in a transaction or implementing a growth strategy. The time, financial and emotional investment can be overwhelming during the preparation and negotiation process, and, because of the perceived urgency and critical nature of the demands, normal management responsibilities often suffer, resulting in slower business development and a lack of cost controls, just to name a few. What can make this issue particularly troublesome in an M&A transaction (or a growth strategy that involves outside funding) is the negative impact to valuation, terms and conditions of a deal if performance begins to slip. Prior to closing, interim financial statements will often be reviewed to measure company results against projections or expectations. Though some slippage is bound to occur due to the dilution of management attention, poor business performance can affect the terms the buyer or funding source originally agreed to. The risk is especially high in situations with a protracted negotiating period.

FINAL THOUGHTS

In the discussion above, we defined the main levers that management of a private, middle-market company can use to increase the return on invested capital, reduce the risk of investment and ease the transfer to new owners for successful M&A transactions and growth initiatives. Two additional influences will likely impact the outcome:

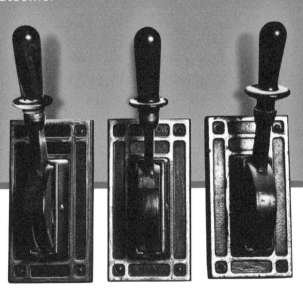

MARKET TIMING

- The level of industry transaction activity can affect value. In a hot and active deal market, management may find it easier to attract capital, investment and buyers at values and terms favorable to the company. Certain industries and sectors experience waves of activity and interest. On the front-end of these cycles, valuations and deal terms will likely favor the seller and can provide an opportunity for owners and management to act to monetize value closer to owner expectations even if the company isn't ready.

COMPETITIVE PROCESS

- The degree of process competition or engagement with multiple bidders is important. The presence of multiple, interested buyers or investors has significant potential positive impact in optimizing the value for a seller or company raising capital and increases the likelihood of closing a transaction.

  Conversely, the buyer or investor who finds proprietary or unique targets and acts quickly can seize valuable opportunities. A well-managed transaction process with the right teammates and advisors acting in accord should prove to be an investment with a return and increase the likelihood of a successful outcome. For many business owners, selling a business or obtaining growth financing is like being on fourth and goal in the final quarter of a football game ... there is no more critical time to execute and to execute well.

As you think about what we have presented, preparing for and optimizing a business in anticipation of M&A and growth takes time and planning. In the public markets, shareholder value is paramount and is legislated as the deciding factor for doing deals. In private, middle-market companies, price goes along with the ambitions and motivations of its owners. The transaction process can be a significant distraction to a company; sufficient preparation that enables management to act quickly and deliberately will have tangible value that should not be underestimated.

Achieving shareholder objectives and the desired deal value requires a careful analysis and positioning in a way that can be done discreetly, with confidence and on the shareholders' terms. Plan ahead.

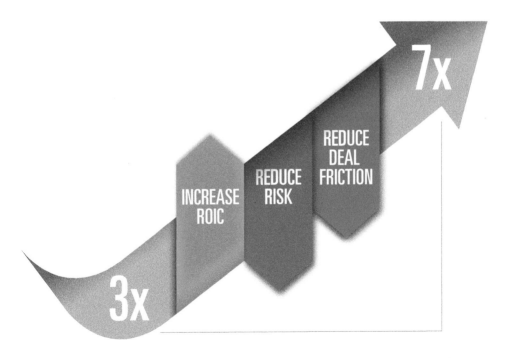

Visit www.ValueLevers.net for additional content and tools.

CHECKLIST OF KEYPOINTS

Increasing ROIC

1. Strategic position
2. Customer base
3. Cost structure & scalability
4. Working capital
5. Human capital

Reducing Risk

1. Awareness & planning
2. Growth plans & relative position
3. Leadership team
4. Predictability of revenues & earnings
5. Concentrations
6. Compliance
7. Keeping current

Easing the Transfer

1. Financial information
2. Contracts
3. Title to assets
4. Corporate structure & attributes
5. The core business
6. Market timing
7. Competitive process

Visit www.ValueLevers.net for additional content and tools.

FORMULA DEFINITIONS

$$VALUE = \frac{expected\ cash\ flow}{cost\ of\ capital - growth\ rate\ of\ the\ cash\ flow}$$

TERM	DEFINITION
value	Enterprise value of the company is equal to the market value of the company's debt and equity
expected cash flow	Future cash flow (normalized, after tax and after capital expenditures but before interest expense) that is expected to be generated by the business to service debt and then be available to shareholders
cost of capital	Weighted average expected return for debt and equity based on the risk and capital structure of the business
Growth rate	The annual rate of growth of the expected cash flow

$$ROIC = \frac{operating\ profit - adjusted\ taxes}{total\ assets - non\text{-}interest\ bearing\ debt}$$

TERM	DEFINITION
operating profit	Normalized earnings before other income, other expenses, interest and taxes
adjusted taxes	Cash payments for corporate income taxes
total assets	Total balance sheet assets using GAAP
Non-interest bearing debt	Liabilities that are not subject to accrued or actual interest (those considered funded debt). Typically this includes accounts payables and accruals

Visit www.ValueLevers.net for additional content and tools.

ABOUT THE AUTHORS

Kenneth H. Marks, CM&AA, CFq

Kenneth is the Founder and Managing Partner of High Rock Partners, a boutique firm of strategic and M&A advisors. He is an entrepreneur and subject matter expert in mergers, acquisitions and financing of emerging growth and middle-market companies. He combines first-hand experiences in financing, building and selling multiple businesses for himself with more than twenty years of developing growth strategies and doing deals. He helps CEOs make key strategic decisions, navigate and execute transitions of ownership, accelerate growth to the next level or reposition the company. His firm uses a unique and proven blend of experiences and tools in strategy, mergers and acquisitions, financing and deals coupled with leadership and creative solutions to achieve his clients' desired outcomes.

Kenneth is the lead author of *Middle Market M&A: Handbook for Investment Banking and Business Consulting* and the *Handbook of Financing Growth: Strategies, Capital Structure and M&A Transactions*, both published by John Wiley & Sons in their Finance Series. He has an electrical engineering background and obtained an MBA from Kenan-Flagler Business School at the University of North Carolina Chapel Hill. Kenneth is a Certified Merger & Acquisition Advisor (CM&AA) and holds a Corporate Finance Qualification (CFq).

John "Buddy" A. Howard, CFA, ASA

Buddy has more than 30 years of experience as a valuation and financial analyst. He has completed more than 200 valuations in a wide variety of industries and has served as an expert witness in the area of business valuation approximately 30 times. Mr. Howard has been ranked in the top 50 M&A advisors based on transaction volume in the banking sector according to *U.S. Banker*.

He has achieved his Chartered Financial Analyst (CFA) designation from the CFA Institute and his Accredited Senior Appraiser designation (ASA) from the American Society of Appraisers. He has held a Series 7 (General Securities), Series 24 (General Securities Principal), and Series 86/87 (Research Analyst) licenses.

OTHER RESOURCES

Kenneth H. Marks is the lead author of *Middle Market M & A: Handbook for Investment Banking and Business Consulting,* 1st Edition, ISBN-10: 0470908297

Kenneth H Marks is the lead author of *The Handbook of Financing Growth: Strategies, Capital Structure, and M&A Transactions,* 2nd Edition, ISBN-10: 0470390158

Visit www.ValueLevers.net for additional content and tools.

REFERENCES

Blees, C., Managing Partners, BiggsKofford Capital, Interview, December 2014

Copeland, T., Koller, T., Murrin, J. (1996). *Valuation: Measuring and Managing the Value of Companies*, 2nd Edition. John Wiley & Sons, Inc. Hoboken, New Jersey.

Damodaran, A. (1999). *Applied Corporate Finance*. John Wiley & Sons, Inc., Hoboken, New Jersey.

Marks, K., Slee, R., Blees, C., & Nall, M. (2012). *Middle Market M&A: Handbook for Investment Banking and Business Consulting*. John Wiley & Sons, Inc., Hoboken, New Jersey.

Sanginario, K., Founder, Corporate Value Metrics, Interview, December 2014

Visit www.ValueLevers.net for additional content and tools.